The Point of Love

Monique Mulligan

Compiled and published by Serenity Press

Copyright © 2016 Serenity Press

All rights reserved. No part of this book may be used or reproduced by any means, graphic, electronic, or mechanical, including photocopying, recording, taping or by any information storage retrieval system without the written permission of the copyright owner except in the case of brief quotations embodied in critical articles and reviews.

Serenity Press books may be ordered through online booksellers or by contacting:
www.serenitypress.org
serenitypress@hotmail.com

Because of the dynamic nature of the Internet, any web addresses or links contained in this book may have changed since publication and may no longer be valid. The views expressed in this work are solely those of the authors and do not necessarily reflect the views of the publisher and the publisher hereby disclaims any responsibility for them.

The author(s) of this book do not dispense medical advice or prescribe the use of any technique as a form of treatment for physical, emotional, or medical problems without the advice of a physician, either directly or indirectly. The intent of the author(s) is only to offer information of a general nature to help you. In the event you use any of the information in this book for yourself, which is your constitutional right, the author(s) and the publisher assume no responsibility for your actions.

ISBN: (sc) 978-0-9944730-9-7

ISBN: (e) 978-0-9945265-1-9

The Point of Love

LEXIE'S phone vibrated on the café table, the alarm indicating she had 20 minutes to get to her next appointment. Her eyes drifted to the Rockingham beachfront, bustling with holiday-makers, and for a moment she wished she could throw off her heels and stick her feet into the glassy water that lapped against the sand. Pushing the thought aside, she faced the two men in suits who shared her table.

'I've got to go. Another job to get to,' she apologised as she gathered her notepad and camera.

'Have you got everything you need?' the older man asked, handing her a pile of glossy marketing information.

'Yes, I do, thanks. I'll call or email if I have any other questions,' she said, shaking both men's hands.

Back in the office, Lexie made a beeline for the senior journalist's desk. Mish, thirty and flirty, had grown up locally and had been working at the paper for several years, whereas Lexie had recently moved to the area from the northern suburbs. She hoped Mish would be able to fill in some gaps about her mid-morning meeting. Lexie suspected the project the men were marketing might be highly controversial. At twenty-six, she was hardly a jaded journalist, but her developing cynic radar told her the meeting reeked of sales pitch.

Mish pulled ear buds from her ear and smiled in greeting. She'd gone out of her way to make Lexie feel welcome and show her the ropes in the busy office.

'How'd the meeting with the Mangles Bay Marina spin doctors go?' Mish asked.

Lexie laughed. Mish's cynic radar was spot on. 'Good. We went to Sunsets. They gave me the rundown on how a marina-based tourist precinct would, and I quote, "transform a degraded parcel of land at Mangles Bay into an asset brimming with economic benefits". Even took me for a drive out there.' She took a breath. 'You know, it's pretty scrubby. And so much rubbish – junk food packaging, plastic bags... even old couches and stuff dumped on the side of the road. Don't people use bins around here?'

'Yeah, some scumbags don't give a toss.' Mish shook her head in disgust. 'There'll be a clean-up organised for the area soon, I think.

The Point of Love

'I was wondering, though...' Lexie rustled through the notepad until she found what she was after. 'A 500-pen marina, room for charter boats, a residential development with restaurants and cafés – it sounds pretty good on paper. Oh, and the nature reserve – which I didn't see – that's also going to be rehabilitated.'

'Sounds like there's a but,' Mish said, waiting.

'You know there is, Mish. On the one hand, it's strange that Rockingham doesn't have a marina. That storm last week ripped boats from their moorings – there's no safe harbour for them. I had all these people come up and tell me about the need for a marina when I was taking photos of the stranded boats on Palm Beach.'

'But?' Mish said again. Her voice was patient, but her eyes flickered back to her computer.

'But why were there signs saying, "Save Point Peron" mounted on the side of the road? What's the story there?'

'A lot of people are against the development – they're worried it's going to become a canal estate. You need to speak to the Hands Off Point Peron group. They'll fill you in.' Mish opened a copy of last week's paper and turned to the Letters to the Editor page. She jabbed her finger on one of the letters. 'Talk to this guy. Andrew Fletcher. He's one of the spokespeople. And he's a sexy beast. I wouldn't mind keeping his mouth busy.'

Lexie spluttered with laughter. Mish never failed to shock her.

'What's going on? Not work from what I can see.' The editor's sour voice interrupted their mirth. John Parker wasted few chances to remind his staff who was boss.

Lexie explained, ignoring the kissing motions Mish was making on her hand behind John's back.

'…and so Mish thought I should have a chat with this guy, Andrew Fletcher. Get some background, maybe a new angle.' She showed John the letter.

John looked as though he'd sucked a lemon.

'Fletcher? He's an arrogant prick. But, since you're new, I suppose it's not a completely stupid idea to meet him.' Behind John's back, Mish rolled her eyes. 'Don't get behind on your other work, though, Alexandra. I've got a bloody paper to fill.' He turned to Mish. 'Don't think I don't know what you're doing back there, Michelle. Saw your reflection in the computer screen.' He stomped away.

As soon as his office door slammed, the two women burst out laughing. When they calmed, after a number of false starts created by Mish re-enacting the scene, Lexie had one more question.

'Why does he hate this Andrew Fletcher so much?'

Mish considered the question. 'Not sure. They went to uni together… but that's all I know.'

The Point Peron car park was deserted when Lexie pulled in. No sign of Andrew Fletcher. A quick glance at her phone reassured her that she was on time – three minutes early in fact – she hated to be late. Grabbing her notebook and camera, she climbed out of her car and leaned against it, taking the opportunity to get her bearings before he arrived.

From the car park, Point Peron didn't look like much. Lexie knew it was a popular fishing and snorkelling spot, but from her vantage point, the scrub-covered limestone didn't look like it was worth the fuss people made. Perhaps the developers were on the money. Turn the area into a tourist hotspot, a destination.

Her mind wandered to Andrew Fletcher and her phone conversation with him yesterday. His voice, a smooth baritone, had conveyed confidence, and a hint of curiosity. Lexie had introduced herself, which prompted a spiel from Fletcher populated with the words 'spin' and 'propaganda'.

She'd interrupted him then, cool but firm.

'Andrew, I haven't lived in the area long, so I'm still getting my head around the issue, but I have to say, it looks good on paper.' She'd held her breath, hoping he wouldn't slam down the phone. It happened sometimes in this business.

He hadn't. Instead, he'd offered to show her Point Peron 'properly', his voice calm, but inviting. Its smooth tone made her think of salted caramel on a bed of vanilla bean ice cream, her favourite dessert. And now here she was. Waiting for him to turn up so she could see whether he looked as good as his voice had sounded.

Lexie's thoughts were interrupted as a car drove in beside her and Thor jumped out. He strode towards her, all six-foot-two rippling muscle and windswept hair in blue jeans.

Am I dreaming? Why is Thor in Rockingham?

'Sorry, I'm late. It's Lexie, right?' Thor stretched out his hand.

Lexie blinked. For once, Mish's judgement was spot on. This Norse god was indeed a sexy beast. Abruptly she gathered herself and stretched out her hand.

'Yes, I'm Lexie. And you're Thor, I mean, Andrew."

Oh God. I called him Thor. I hope he didn't hear that.

Andrew lifted his eyebrows as he shook her hand.

Oh God. He did. Could this be any more embarrassing?

'Right. So, do you want to do the photo or tour first?'

'Uh, photo,' Lexie said, trying to regain control of the situation.

Get a grip. You have a job to do.

'Do you have anywhere in mind?' Andrew asked. Was he smirking?

'Well, as you know, I haven't been here before.' Lexie couldn't stop the hint of defensiveness that crept into her voice. She seemed to be apologising about that a lot lately. 'I moved here about a month ago. I'm still getting my bearings around this place. Last week I accidently left a man waiting on the beach for two hours because I was waiting at the wrong car park. I thought he'd ditched the interview so I went back to the office. He was so cranky when I finally caught up with him and really sunburnt…'

The Point of Love

She trailed off. What was wrong with her? She wasn't easily flustered most of the time. She'd interviewed plenty of cute guys before and she hadn't behaved like a giddy teenager. Something about Andrew had her all in a tizz, and it wasn't only his close resemblance to Thor. This would not do. She had to get a hold of herself. Now. It didn't help that he was assessing her with piercing blue eyes that felt like they were reading her mind.

'Okay. How about we start with the scenic tour, then the photo?' he offered.

'That'd be great,' she said, looking at her phone. 'I've got to be back at the office by one, though.'

'Follow me.' Andrew led the way to a set of stairs. 'We'll go up to the World War II observation post first.'

Lexie followed Andrew, trying not to look at the curve of his butt in his jeans, and trying harder to keep up with his long strides. It wasn't easy, considering she was wearing a new pair of heels. At the base of the stairs, he stopped and faced Lexie.

'Are you sure you'll be right to climb these stairs in those shoes? There's seventy-one of them – it's a bit of a climb. I'm used to it – come down here a couple of mornings a week to run up them – but those shoes could make it a bit hard going.'

Seriously? You run up those stairs? Who does that?

Lexie lifted her chin. 'I'll be fine, thanks. Shall we go?'

He shrugged and turned towards the stairs, but not before she saw a smile curve his lips. He didn't waste any more time, taking two steps at a time on his way up.

She set off up the limestone stairs as gracefully as she could manage in two-inch heels, grateful that he was looking straight ahead, intent on his goal, and not able to see her face twist in a grimace every time she stumbled on a loose stone. At least it wasn't windy; she had enough to carry without worrying about her skirt flying up.

Halfway up, she stopped to catch her breath. Her face was hot and sweat pooled stickily under her arms. She hoped wet patches weren't showing through her shirt. The last time she'd felt this puffed was during a netball game with her friends, years ago. She'd resembled a boiled beetroot that day, too.

'You okay?' Andrew called down.

Lexie lifted her camera to her face and looked through the viewfinder, trying to slow her breathing.

'Fine,' she called back. 'I'm… um… taking a photo.'

Great. All I can see is the car park. Well, he doesn't know that. Fake it.

Three minutes later, she reached the top, where Andrew was leaning against the fence.

'You get some good shots?'

'Mmm-hmm,' she said, still unable to talk.

'Nice car park, isn't it?'

Her eyes met his, taking in what most definitely looked like a twinkle.

Oh god. He's taking the piss.

The Point of Love

Before she could answer, he pointed at something beyond them.

'Look. Check out the view.'

She looked. And saw a panorama of coastal landscape, with long stretches of sand curving around a series of bays, hugging a group of rocky islands and one larger island.

'It's so beautiful,' she breathed, forgetting her embarrassment of a moment earlier.

'That's Shoalwater Islands Marine Park. It's a protected marine sanctuary that covers more than six thousand hectares, stretching from Point Becher near Port Kennedy and up to here. Look,' he pointed, 'the marine park includes those islands. The big one's Penguin Island, which is home to a colony of Little Penguins. This colony has the highest conservation status of all penguin colonies in Australia.'

'I didn't know that.' Lexie scrabbled in her bag for her pen and notebook, shifting her camera strap over her shoulder.

'It's not only the penguins that are significant here,' Andrew continued when she was ready. 'The whole marine park is home to an abundance of seabirds, many of which are hardly ever seen on the mainland. Sixteen species use those islands for courtship, breeding, nesting and feeding. Out there,' he pointed to a smaller, rocky outcrop, 'that's Seal Island, which is home to a colony of Australian sea lions. They are the rarest species in the world and they are highly protected. Surrounding the area are reefs, which support a host of temperate and subtropical invertebrates.'

'Invertebrates? Like, sea stars?'

'Yes, and urchins and molluscs. And of course, there are dolphins and a number of fish species.'

Lexie did her best to keep up as Andrew continued his run-down of the marine park's significance, asking the odd question when she could get a word in. Her questions about how the development proposals would impact on the park could wait. His love for the area was obvious. Passion underlined his words and she could see some great quotes emerging.

I love his voice. I could listen to it all day.

'Lexie?'

She jumped.

'I said, do you want to see the lookout? It's a good spot for photos.'

'Lead the way,' she smiled.

That way I can watch you walk.

On the way to the lookout, Andrew pointed out the remains of military gun placements and bunkers, explaining that they formed part of a World War II coastal defence strategy.

'We were just standing at the observation post,' he told her as they walked. 'This is all that's left and it's not in great condition. Bloody vandals keep trashing the place. Needs to be restored, the historical value of the place preserved.'

The Point of Love

'Aren't all the gun placements connected by a series of tunnels under the dunes?' she asked, recalling an article she'd read.

Andrew nodded.

'They are. So many people around here have no idea these remains exist, that this site was an integral part of border protection during the war. Luckily, the reservists have come on board and they're helping restore the infrastructure, starting with digging out some of the dirt and sand that's built up. About time, too. And there's talk of a museum, which would be great. It'll help tell a story that's been almost forgotten.'

She was beginning to see why Andrew was so enthralled by the area.

They reached the lookout, and while Andrew was staring down at the sea-worn rocks, she took the chance to rub her aching feet. Blisters had already formed on her toes and heels, and she wished she could plunge her feet into the healing salt water below. Her shoes were back on before he turned, motioning her to the edge of the lookout.

He pointed out Garden Island and the causeway; she listened with rapt attention as he recalled days of snorkelling in the small rocky bays below, scribbling down notes as she went. It sounded idyllic. Picnics, swimming, snorkelling... Lexie wasn't a big fan of beach swimming, but she'd happily get used to it if Andrew was her guide.

Her phone beeped, announcing a message from Mish: **Where r u? John wants 2 have staff meeting in 45.**

'I've got to go,' Lexie said, regretfully. 'There's a meeting I have to be at. Can I take a photo?'

Preferably sans shirt.

'Where do you want me?' Andrew was all seriousness.

Anywhere.

The second Lexie lifted the camera to her face, a gust of wind swept in from the ocean, swirling under her skirt. In a fit of mischief, the wind shot the summery fabric skyward and gave Andrew a view of her red lace undies that were better suited to a bedroom than a beach. If a sinkhole could have opened under her feet and sucked her into the sand, Lexie would have welcomed it.

Heat rushed to her cheeks. She couldn't hold her skirt and the camera at the same time so she clicked away, capturing Andrew's reactions to the wind's merry dance with her skirt. His mouth made a surprised 'O' and his cheeks flushed, then his gaze dropped to her legs and shot back up again. When he finally looked at her directly, the heat in his gaze made her knees wobble.

'Have you got what you need?' His voice was husky and as she lowered the camera, his eyes melted her.

'Um, no, I mean yes,' she said, stumbling over her words. What was it with this guy?

'Let's get back then,' he said, suddenly all business, turning to look over the ocean.

Disappointment flowed through her. She was not sure why the mood shift mattered so much. Questions competed for first place in her racing mind. Had she been mistaken?

The Point of Love

Was she kidding herself? The way he'd looked at her a moment ago, she'd been sure there was a spark of something between them and now he couldn't seem to get away fast enough. Then again, they *had* just met. Maybe she was reading more into it – he might have liked what he saw, but that was it. From what she knew of guys, red lace was a pretty universal eye-catcher. Not that she was a great judge of guys. Her last boyfriend had turned out to be the cheater of cheaters.

She pulled off her heels and hurried along, trying to keep up with long legs encased in tight blue jeans, and a butt that was— *Enough!* Her mind was all over the place, re-living the scene at the lookout while trying to read what Andrew was thinking. She didn't need Andrew's butt confusing things further. She caught up and walked beside him the last few steps to the car park. If only he would say something. He said nothing, but looked her way a couple of times, his expression inscrutable. It was doing her head in.

At the car park, Lexie held out her hand, once more the professional journalist. She hoped Andrew would overlook her bare feet and chipped toe polish, and groaned inwardly when he looked down. A slight frown crossed his face. She squared her shoulders, resolving to keep a more sensible pair of shoes in the car from now on. He probably thought she was a ditz.

'Thanks for your time, Andrew,' she said, looking him in the eye, her back straight. If he could be all business, so could she. 'If I've got any more questions can I flick you a quick email?'

'Sure.' He shook her hand. His hand was warm and felt like it belonged in hers. 'Will I see a copy of the article before it goes to print?'

'Sorry, no. It's not common practice to do that,' she explained. 'But if I can't read my own writing, I'll be sure to check any quotes with you.'

He nodded. His hand lingered in hers. 'I'll see you, then.'

It was her turn to smile. 'You might want to let go of my hand.'

Or not. I'm happy with that.

'Right.' He let go and instantly her hand felt cold, and strangely alone.

Her phone beeped with another message from Mish. What was so important?

'I've really got to get back to the office,' Lexie said, opening the car door and shoving her belongings on the passenger seat, before sliding into the car.

'Me too. See you and um, thanks.'

His next words came out in a rush.

'I was wondering, that is, since you don't know the area well, if you'd like a tour of Penguin Island?'

Lexie sucked in her breath. Was he asking her on a date? Or was this business?

'For a story, you mean? Because if it is, I'd have to check with the editor. And I'd need an angle.'

'No! I mean, no, not for a story. I wondered if you'd like to, well, we could bring a picnic, there's no café there, but if maybe you'd like to go as... a sort of date.' He blushed, hope softening his features.

Gone was Mr All Business. Lexie liked the vulnerability she saw on his face. He was really quite cute when he blushed and stammered. She wouldn't mind kissing those flushed cheeks... or those ever-so-slightly trembling lips.

'Sort of?' she teased.

He laughed. 'God, I don't know what it is about you, but I'm acting like a teenager.' He leaned towards the window, suddenly serious. 'A real date. You and me.'

'I'd love to.' The words were out there before Lexie could think about them. Instead, her thoughts were on the distance between his lips and hers.

He grinned. 'I'll call you to make a time. You'd better go. And soak those feet or something. I didn't realise they were so blistered.'

He patted the roof of her car, stepped back and watched as she drove away.

After a run of stinking hot days, Lexie was pleased to see the onset of an early sea breeze on Saturday morning. The air carried the tang of salt, a briny flavour typical of the coastal location. Temperatures hovering in the high thirties had kept her indoors the past few days, with stagnant, heavy nights failing to entice her out of the air-conditioning. She was itching for some fresh air and by the looks of it, it was perfect picnic weather.

Andrew had phoned the evening after their meeting at Point Peron, with a proposal to picnic on the island that Saturday if she was free. Lexie hoped he didn't think she was lame or desperate for having no plans other than washing and grocery shopping, but it was a sad fact. She'd moved to Rockingham for her job and had yet to establish a network of friends; her hours were often long, and all too often, her weekends were spent catching up with things she'd missed on account of work.

To say she was excited to see somewhere different – not to mention a date with a Thor lookalike – was an understatement. Like a child on Christmas morning, she bounced out of bed with uncharacteristic energy. Not a morning person, she battled with the snooze button most days. By eight-thirty she'd showered, shaved and moisturised her legs, painted her toenails, tried on and discarded numerous outfits, packed a bag with sunscreen, a towel, bottled water and a hat, and cleaned her small apartment. Realising she had an hour and a half to kill, she pottered about, laughing at a barrage of texts from Mish containing helpful advice and pictures of Thor.

Finally, it was time to leave. Grabbing her keys and bag, Lexie gave herself a final once over before locking up, then ran out to her car. Driving along Safety Bay Road to Pengos Café, she tried to ignore the fluttering of her stomach, the self-doubt that lurked beneath her excitement. It had been a long time between dates.

Be confident, be yourself. He's just a guy. Except he's not just a guy. He's Thor. Well, not Thor, but nearly. And I really like him. And for some reason, I really want him to like me.

Luck was on her side in the car park, with a car space vacated as Lexie pulled off Arcadia Drive. She took a moment to collect herself and then stepped out. *Here goes.*

'Over here, Lexie.' Andrew was waiting on the grassed area to the side of the café. He looked cool and hot at the same time in a slim-fit tee and cut-offs. *How does he do that?*

'Thor! I mean, Andrew, I *thought* that was you,' she said, groaning inwardly at her mistake. She had to get the Thor image out of her head, once and for all. She went on, hoping to distract him: 'Have you been waiting long?'

'No,' he said. 'Only a few minutes.'

'Shall we go and get tickets?'

'All sorted.' He tapped his shirt pocket.

'Very organised,' she said, impressed.

He grinned. 'Wait till you see the picnic. Come on, let's go catch that ferry.'

The ferry was packed with day-trippers this time of the day, although a few intrepid souls were attempting the walk over the sandbar in defiance of warning signs. Lexie had read that the widows of two men who'd drowned making the crossing some years earlier had recently received compensation, and couldn't help wonder why people still chose to walk over. Andrew followed her gaze.

'They'll be okay this morning,' he said. 'This afternoon, it'll be different. They'll need to catch the ferry back. I hope they're smart enough to realise that. The ferry operators have to rescue so many people who don't think about how the conditions change. Or ignore sandbar closures.'

'Have you ever walked over?'

'Yeah. I grew up here. My dad taught me what to look out for. But, it's risky if you don't know what you're doing, and while it might look okay on the surface, it's not always safe.'

Lexie nodded. She wasn't planning on taking that risk at all.

Andrew touched her arm briefly. 'Don't worry. I'm setting a good example these days.'

'Good to hear.' *Now bring your hand back.*

Moments later, they stepped off the ferry and onto the jetty.

'Lead the way,' she said, lightly. 'I'm all yours.'

God. That came out wrong. Maybe he won't notice.

'Is that so? Nice to know.'

'I didn't mean…'

'I know. But you're very cute when you blush. Which you appear to do a lot.'

With you around, I sure do.

'I seem to have rendered you speechless,' he added.

'You seem to have that effect on me,' she countered.

The banter continued as Andrew and Lexie toured the island, bypassing the Discovery Centre where tourists could watch a penguin feeding session in favour of a less-crowded walk around the nature reserve. Though they kept to the paths, nesting seabirds squawked indignantly whenever Lexie and Andrew stopped for too long – him pointing out the different types of birds and her content to lean close and listen. Between the fresh sea breeze, the waves slapping against the sand and rocks, and the birds' cacophony, it was hard to hear.

Lexie had no idea she'd been living so close to this coastal gem. Not only was it pretty, with its sparkling aquamarine waters and windswept beaches, but it was teeming with life, in and out of the water. Lizards played hide and seek in the scrub, pelicans surfed on the wind, cormorants dried their wings after fishing, and seagulls bickered without drawing breath; a couple of dolphins frolicked in the waves, nervous crabs scuttled under rocks, and a lone sea lion sun-baked on the far side of the island. Lexie felt like a little girl listing all the things she'd seen in one small space. But one thing was missing.

'Where are all the Little Penguins?' Lexie asked. Andrew had spread out a picnic blanket and was now unpacking the perfect marketing package for south-west produce: locally-produced olives, cheeses, stuffed peppers, crackers, bread and even a bottle of wine.

He laughed. 'I was wondering when you'd ask that. They're shy little things and it can be hard to spot them in the wild, but anyway, during the day this time of the year, you'd be hard pressed to because they'll be feeding in the waters around the marine park. In winter, they're here nesting, but the island's closed then to give them some peace.'

Lexie tried not to look disappointed. She'd half expected to see penguins waddling around, showing off in a cute and friendly manner.

'Don't worry,' Andrew added. 'We'll stop by the Discovery Centre before we go so you can see some up close. Now, lunch is served. Hope you like cheese and wine. Thought I'd treat you to some delights of the south-west.'

Does that include you?

He met her eyes with a gaze that seared her soul.

Did I say that out loud? Tell me I didn't.

She waited for him to say something, hoping he put her flushed cheeks down to the fresh air, and praying he couldn't hear her heart thumping. He swallowed and took a deep breath.

'Can I ask you something? Did you call me Thor? The other day when we met?'

Oh God. He did hear that.

'Yes. Yes, I did.'

'I thought so.' He suppressed a smile. 'It's very flattering, of course, but…'

'But?'

'I'm a much better kisser.'

Her heart tap-danced in her chest as her mind processed his unexpected words. Andrew closed the space between them, smooth and sure, leaving no room for doubt.

Pushing wayward strands of hair aside, he cupped her face with his hands, pulled her close, and met her mouth with soft lips tasting of dark chocolate, berries and wine.

The Point of Love

His touch sent a shiver to her toes and he answered by pulling her closer, deepening the kiss. She drank him in, lost in his taste, smell and the stirrings of her body in response to him.

Children's voices, high-pitched and excited, followed by running footsteps and the squawk of indignant sea gulls signalled imminent company.

Andrew pulled away, his breath uneven, and locked his eyes on hers, his gaze a slow burn.

'That,' he said, 'is just a taste.'

It hadn't taken Lexie long to work out that Mondays were hell in the newspaper office. In theory, Mondays were a lunch-at-the-desk, do-not-disturb-I'm-writing day, with John sequestered in his office, and only emerging with bluster to urge the reporters to write more, write faster. Reality told a different story. From last-minute news stories to stories suddenly becoming old news and needing an update, from PR representatives who delayed sending in council comments to ads dropping out and leaving space to fill, something always made deadline day a headache. Like the meeting John had demanded in a voice that did not bode well.

'What have you got for the front page?' It was crunch time.

Lexie, Mish and Brian, another journalist, looked at one another, willing someone to speak up first. Brian cleared his throat.

'The new shopping centre at W—'

'No. Next.'

Mish shuffled through her notepad.

'Neighbour feud over missing cats. Man pulled over for speeding, turned out to be naked.'

Brian stifled a laugh. John glared at him and then at Mish.

'You think it's fucking funny? I've got a bloody front page to fill and there's stuff all in the files. And you lot come up with shopping centres, missing cats and naked bloody drivers. You'll all be coming up with new jobs if I don't have something in here by the end of lunch.'

Lexie avoided eye contact with her colleagues. It had been a particularly slow news week, with most of her jobs tending toward soft news side – lifestyle and picture stories. Mish had complained about the lack of good – or bad, depending on how one looked at it – police news leads, while Brian hadn't been able to come up with anything hard hitting in his industry round.

'You.' John thrust a finger at Lexie. 'You've been faffing about with the Mangles Bay lot and mooning over bloody Fletcher – yes, I've heard about it – but all you've come up with is,' he jabbed at a print-out of Lexie's story, 'this Hands Off Point Peron update. Boring. Turn *this* into a front pager. Think of the storm last week, the boats that washed up. There's your angle – residents' plea for fast-tracking the marina. Give the piece some guts.'

He sighed and turned to his computer, muttering: 'Bloody spoon-feeding, that's what this is.'

Brian coughed. John wheeled around in his chair.

The Point of Love

'Well? What are you lot sitting here for? Go.'

Back at her desk, Lexie stared blankly at her notes. It was her first front page opportunity but she couldn't summon up any excitement. How was she supposed to make this a lead story? In three hours? She barely had her head around the issue as it was, and now she was supposed to track down some residents and get their views? Impossible. It didn't help that since meeting Andrew she'd started to question the development, and she knew enough to say fast-tracking the project was not the answer.

And then she saw it – a different angle, buried in Andrew's letter to the editor. He'd asked about the full-cost benefit of the Mangles Bay project, concerned that the developer was withholding information that was in the public's interest to know. Had the council demanded full financial information from the developer? If not, why not? And why hadn't the developers released the full information?

An hour later, she'd sent questions to the council and the developer's media liaison officers with a clear deadline for responses, and sketched the basis for her story. To appease John, she'd called a couple of marina-supporting residents – thanks to Mish for coming up with some names – and had some quotes in a separate draft. Her hope was that she wouldn't need them.

By five o'clock she'd submitted her story to John; she'd managed to fend him off for a couple of hours, and he was too distracted to notice. A lack of response from the council and developer meant she'd had to tack on a 'did not respond to questions by deadline', but overall, she was pleased with her effort. By six-fifteen she was on her way home, satisfied with getting through another deadline day and ready for a glass of wine.

If only Andrew was there to share it with me.

Lexie woke with the feeling she hadn't had enough sleep. The night had been hot and sticky and every time she threw her sheet off, the breeze from the fan made her cold again. It had taken her ages to fall asleep, with her thoughts alternating between Andrew and anticipation about seeing the newspaper's front page. When she finally fell asleep she dreamed of Thor wrapping his arms around her and drawing her in for a lingering kiss, their hips pressing together, breathing faster… until John turned up and started yelling about a naked man on a stranded boat in the middle of the shopping centre.

Bloody John, ruining my dream when it was getting to the good bit.

'Well,' she told herself as she readied herself for work, 'today's an easy day and you've got tonight to look forward to.' Andrew had called the evening before and invited her to dinner at Rustico, a popular tapas bar on the foreshore. She hadn't seen him since their picnic at Penguin Island, as he had a prior commitment on the Sunday; she felt like pressing fast-forward on the day to bring their date closer. It was crazy: she'd met Andrew not even a week ago, yet her whole being felt alive and full of joy just at the

The Point of Love

thought of him. She was looking forward to discussing her article with him, too.

Her phone rang as she was driving to work and Lexie brightened when Andrew's voice filled the car. Except, it didn't sound warm and sexy like it had last night; this morning it was curt, with an edge of anger.

'What the hell is that story?' There was no 'hello'.

'What? You've seen it already? What's wrong with it?' Lexie felt like she'd started a race two minutes too late and had no chance of catching up.

'Got a copy from the deli. Wanted to see the front page. You've made me look like an idiot.' He hung up.

Lexie was stunned. What was Andrew talking about?

Why would I make him look like an idiot? Why? And how?

She slammed her hand on the steering wheel in frustration, willing the traffic to move faster so she could get to work and try to figure out what had Andrew so pissed off. A mixture of helplessness and defensiveness prompted the sting of tears: she hadn't even *seen* the front page yet and she was getting attitude. And there was nothing she could do until she got to work. *If* she ever got to work. Obviously, she'd missed the memo that it was Drive Like A Snail day.

Her dark mood was not missed by the receptionist, who raised her eyebrows when Lexie slammed through the front door, snatched up a newspaper and strode into the office minus her usual friendly greeting. Oblivious to the 'Morning Lexie' called out by other staff, her eyes scanned the front page, noting the picture of a resident standing beside a stranded boat – one she'd taken the previous week but not used – and the pun-laden headline: "Aboat time". The subheading was equally bad: "Stop the waddle: residents apply pier pressure."

As she started reading the article, Lexie's brow furrowed, shoulders tensed and her fingers gripped the newspaper like talons on helpless prey. She wanted to tear her precious front page story to shreds and compost it in John's mouth. John had edited the last-minute quotes she'd collected from boat owners the day before but stored in draft. They'd been built around a tongue-in-cheek quote from Andrew: 'I'm standing up for the little guy – the Little Penguins who can't speak up for themselves. And if that means the marina misses the boat, good.'

It was not the article she'd submitted. And it did make Andrew look like an idiot.

'Shit!' She cursed louder than intended, but ignored the raised eyebrows and sideways glances of her colleagues.

Out of the corner of her eye, she saw John sneak into his office. Before he could shut the door, she was in there, barely reining in the urge to throw the newspaper at her boss's head.

'What the hell is this? I didn't write this! It's not the front page story I submitted!' She spat out her words in a rush, her voice laced with anger and protectiveness.

John closed the door, faced her and folded his arms. There was no hint of remorse in his eyes.

The Point of Love

'Your story was shite—'

'Are you serious?' she interrupted. 'It was a *good* story – it's in the public interest to know the full cost of this development …'

'It was not balanced. No comments from council or the developer. Fletcher's opinion only – that's not enough for a lead. *And* I asked you to write about residents wanting action in light of the storms.' His eyes and voice sang a chorus of defiance.

'The fact that there was no comment *is* of interest. People *should* be wondering why so much is not being said!'

'Yes, but what you came up with was good for a secondary, not for the lead. Look, I needed a strong lead, with a picture to match. Not a bloody pin-up of Fletcher rattling on about birds.'

This time it was even harder to resist shoving the newspaper in his face.

'But this… I didn't write this… tabloid fodder. *You* wrote it, using my draft notes for a different story. You've taken Andrew's words completely out of context – in fact, that quote wasn't even in my story, it was in my notes – and you've put *my* name on it. You've made it into a piece of sensationalist crap—'

She stopped, willing tears not to fall. Not now. Not when John was looking like a thunderous arsehole.

'Enough. At the end of the day, I'm the editor, Lexie. The front page has got to attract readers from headline to visual and all I've done is made sure that happens. Think of this as a learning curve.'

Only the insistent ringing of John's phone stopped Lexie from saying more. Defeated for now, she walked out of the office, mobile phone in hand. She had to call Andrew and explain what had happened. He didn't answer. His phone didn't even go to voicemail so she couldn't leave a message. She tried calling the university where he worked as a research associate, but was stonewalled by one of his colleagues. By the time Mish came to find her, bearing a cup of tea and a worried look, Lexie was unable to hold back her tears. It was another fifteen minutes before she could compose herself enough to return to her desk, avoiding looking in John's direction. Thankfully, he had the good sense to stay clear.

She tapped out an email to Andrew explaining the situation and asked him to call. For the rest of the day, she existed on hope that he would read her email, jumping to attention every time she heard the tell-tale chime of an email landing in her inbox.

His silence was crushing.

The next few days were awful. Lexie received several angry phone calls from supporters of Andrew and of the Hands Off Point Peron project. She tried to phone Andrew a few more times, but by the third day, resigned herself to the fact that he wanted nothing to do with her. Dealing with people's criticism and Andrew's silence had drained her, and stripped away her usual zest for life.

The Point of Love

By the sound of it, John hadn't fared so well, either. He hadn't said anything, but Lexie heard rumblings that a retraction had been requested. She didn't question him and kept to herself, autopilot keeping her on task. When the council submitted its response to her questions about the financial costs of the Mangles Bay project, full of words that said nothing at all, she updated her story and re-submitted it without a word.

At night, she watched mindless TV before reading in bed, trying to keep her mind from Andrew, the story and a phone that didn't ring. It didn't work; each morning she woke exhausted from the effort her body was putting into over-analysing their conversations, the story, Andrew's angry response... and the melting kiss they had shared that still made her heart beat faster at the memory. Lexie had been kissed before, but not like this; Andrew's kisses spoke of possibility, not only of desire, but of the beginning of something that mattered. Too bad it was over before it got started.

It was Mish who finally snapped Lexie out of her melancholy.

'Why aren't you angry?' Mish threw this at Lexie while they were waiting in line at the coffee van visiting the office.

'With John? What do you think?' Irritation flared in Lexie's voice, a combination of tiredness and annoyance at the reminder of John's actions.

'No, with Andrew. The guy hasn't even let you explain.' Mish swore, causing the coffee man to look at her in surprise. She flashed a flirtatious smile at the man and placed her hand on his arm. 'Not you, handsome. Another guy.' He blushed and dropped the sugar container, spilling sachets on to the ground.

Mish turned back to Lexie, the coffee man forgotten.

'Look, Andrew's got a right to be pissed about the article. But you've tried to explain what really happened and Mr I'm-So-Hot can't be stuffed listening. And you're taking it. If it was me, I'd be furious. Two flat whites, please.' She beamed at the coffee man, who had given up on the sugar sachets and was openly listening.

'What good's that going to do? Being furious? Sure, I wanted to explain, to defend myself, and I've tried, Mish. I've called him, I've emailed him. But if he doesn't want to hear it... what am I supposed to do?' Lexie was genuinely confused. She dug in her purse to find some change for the coffee, but Mish waved her money away.

'My shout. Find another bloke, for starters. He might be hot and kiss like a god, but if he's going to act like this? Toss the jerk, *I* reckon.' She took a breath and changed tack, her voice suddenly cajoling. 'From the way you told it, you guys had something going. Doesn't that deserve more? Some respect, maybe? Communication *both* ways?'

Lexie sipped at the coffee Mish handed her. She was right. Whatever Andrew made of it, whether or not he believed her, she deserved to defend herself. She'd been moping about him for days, but if she'd been right in thinking there was something between them, Lexie wanted a second chance.

The Point of Love

'I've got an idea,' Mish said. 'I reckon you should turn up at the Hands Off Point Peron community forum instead of me tomorrow night. He'll be there for sure.'

Lexie sucked in her breath.

'I don't think so, Mish.'

And yet, despite it all, I want to see him.

Mish grasped Lexie by the shoulders, somehow managing not to spill her coffee.

'Think again, Lexie. It's perfect. *You* get to prove to the supporters and Andrew that you're a balanced reporter. And you can confront him after it's over.' Mish made it sound so reasonable. So easy.

'Confrontation's not really my thing, Mish. I hate it.'

An exaggerated facepalm was Mish's response. 'Woman, you've got to stand up for yourself some time. At least try.'

Lexie breathed out deeply, letting go of fear and welcoming strength.

Mish had a point. And she was going to take it.

Determination, enthusiasm and passion rippled through the crowd at the Rockingham foreshore. Protestors of all ages waved home-made signs reading "Save our future" and "Hands Off Point Peron"; other signs were more political in nature, with the Premier copping more than a few felt-pen jabs. People collected around displays outlining the protestors' alternative plan for a coastal park and raising awareness of Rockingham's Little Penguins. A few tourists watched curiously as the supporters greeted each other, a sea of colourful t-shirts and bobbing cardboard signs uniting in a common cause.

When a singer stepped on to the stage and revved up the crowd with a nostalgic and catchy tribute to growing up in the area, Lexie took notes and snapped photos; for a few moments, Andrew slipped from her mind, as she focused on capturing the mood of the event. But then he was back in her thoughts, with Lexie scanning the crowd for his face.

There he is. God, he's cute.

He was standing to one side, talking intently to a wannabe politician Lexie recognised. She watched him for a moment, her anger fading and admiration rising in its place. His passion for the cause was evident in his face, his gestures and his stance… Lexie couldn't take her eyes off him. Only the beep of her phone made her look down.

Don't let Thor's tight t-shirt make you forget to stand up for yourself.

Lexie laughed. So Mish had come down after all. She looked around and saw Mish standing next to a blonde surfer-type, waiting for Lexie to notice her. Lexie waved, shaking her head at the bossy finger waggle she received in reply. Taking a deep breath, she willed her heart to stop pounding and took a step in Andrew's direction.

He turned. Looked right at her, his eyes widening with some emotion Lexie couldn't quite identify. Lifting her shoulders, she walked up to him, hoping her body language conveyed more confidence than she felt. He made his excuses to the political hopeful and faced her, his eyes searching.

The Point of Love

'Lexie—'

His words were cut off abruptly when someone shouldered past Lexie, knocking her forward and into Andrew's chest. Time stopped as she registered his warm, male scent, his thumping heartbeat, the solid feel of his chest beneath her cheek, and then his arms steadied her, gently setting her back on her feet. The look on his face made her want to kiss him and slap him at the same time.

'If you wanted a hug, you only had to ask,' he said.

'You're very funny,' she shot back, smoothing her skirt, which had somehow ridden higher up her thighs than she would have liked. She straightened, feeling a seed of pleasure as she caught him looking at her legs.

You're mad at him, remember.

She opened her mouth to speak, but he beat her to it, his voice rough with uncertainty.

'I read your email this afternoon. I've been away with work. That oil spill up near Geraldton. I was going to call you tonight, after this. To apologise.'

Too stunned to speak, she waited. She hadn't expected him to make the first move. It had thrown her off balance. He took her hands in his.

'Lexie. I'm sorry I ignored your calls on Monday. I was angry. The article... it was completely the opposite of what I expected. That headline, the sensationalised story... it made me look like such an idiot. And I couldn't figure out why you'd do that. Didn't want to know at first, honestly.'

'I didn't,' she put in.

'I know. I know that now.'

He fell silent. She looked away, trying to gather her thoughts. Questions swirled in her head, mixing with the possibilities that had reignited as soon his hands wrapped around hers.

'Mate? Been looking for you. It's time. Need you to get up on stage.' A young man clapped his hand on Andrew's shoulder.

Andrew released her hands.

'Got to go. Can we talk later?' His face was hopeful.
She nodded.

'Meet me here after the protest? An hour?'

She nodded again and was rewarded with a smile before he jogged over to the stage.

'Woman, if you don't plan on keeping that mouth busy, let me know.' Mish joined Lexie as soon as Andrew walked away, making an exaggerated wink-wink-nudge-nudge face when Lexie looked at her quizzically.

'Not a chance.'

'What did he say?'

'Sorry. He said sorry. For ignoring my calls. He was pretty pissed off at the article and at me... I can understand that. Bloody John,' she paused and shook her head at the memory of the headline, before continuing. 'So, he apologised for not giving me the chance to talk. And he only read my email today because he was away with work because of that oil spill.'

'Of course, the oil spill. He's a marine scientist or something like that, right?'

The Point of Love

'Yeah. Anyway he didn't get to say much more because he had to go up on... look, there he is now.'

They stopped talking as Andrew thanked the supporters and delivered a rousing speech about the group's alternative plan for the area around Point Peron. He was an eloquent speaker, with an ability to command the crowd's attention. Lexie reluctantly shifted her mind to work mode and jotted down quotes for a follow-up article.

'He's good,' Mish said, her eyes fixed on the stage. 'And the fact that he's hot doesn't hurt.'

'Oi. Eyes off.' Lexie smiled, but her message was clear.

Mish raised her eyebrows, a slight smile playing at the corner of her mouth.

'You've got it bad. Real bad. Well, he's all yours. Not my type. Too political. Besides, I've got a date with surfer-boy over there.'

She walked away, leaving Lexie to her note-taking and the knowledge that once again, Mish was right.

I've got it bad. And Hands Off isn't going to be an option for us, if I can help it.

By the time Andrew had managed to make his way over to Lexie, it was eight o'clock. She hadn't minded waiting. Instead, she'd chatted to people who readily shared their views on the Mangles Bay Marina plan, the Hands Off Point Peron alternative vision, and the 'tick and flick' approach they believed was applied in the environmental approval process. It had been an educational evening, professionally and personally, leaving Lexie with a wider understanding of the issue and a lot to think about. But as people drifted away, Lexie's thoughts turned to Andrew.

She shivered. It wasn't cold. The absence of a sea breeze that afternoon had kept temperatures in the high twenties after sunset, promising a sticky night ahead. She recognised the shiver as a sweet and sour cocktail of anticipation and nerves. What was going to happen next? Would Andrew and she be able to move on? Was there an Andrew and Lexie at all?

'You're cold?' Andrew appeared next to Lexie, his question carrying a note of concern.

No, but you can put your arms around me if you like.

'No… not cold.'

She changed the subject, and nodded towards now-empty stage. 'That went well.'

'It did. Lots of new people. More than last time. It's good.'

He waved at a few straggling supporters, then turned his gaze on her, blue eyes whispering over her face.

'Do you want to go get a coffee? Tea? A couple of places are still open.'

'Sure.'

They walked to Rustico, the tapas bar they'd planned to meet at before everything went wrong, and settled at an outside table. Despite the hour, the bar was still half full, and they agreed it would be difficult to talk inside. The next few minutes were taken up with ordering coffee and a selection of tapas, followed by small talk about the heat and the bar, which had won a number of Gold Plate Awards. Finally, Lexie couldn't wait anymore. She had to know what was going on.

'Why didn't you give me a chance to explain?' Lexie blurted out the words.

Andrew looked taken aback. She ploughed on.

'On Monday. I hadn't even seen the article when you called me, and when I realised what had happened, you wouldn't take my calls. I know you said you're sorry, but it hurt. And I just wanted to let you know. Because I thought we had something, and if we're going to *have* something, we've got to be able to listen to each other.' She stopped, aware that she was venturing into babbling territory again. And maybe, she was assuming too much. Maybe there wasn't going to be a something. A tear slid down her cheek and she turned away, embarrassed.

'You're right.' His voice was soft. Gentle. He moved his chair around so they were side-by-side and put his hand on her arm. When she lifted her face to his, he spoke again.

'I should have given you a chance to explain. I was hurt, angry. I acted like a child, jumping to conclusions and having a tantrum. I'm sorry, Lexie. You deserved the right of reply and I didn't give you that.'

She nodded, looked out toward the beach and made a decision. It was time to move this on.

'I get why you were angry. I do. I was angry, too. Had a huge bust-up with John about it.'

'Parker does bring that out in people.' At her quizzical look, he continued. 'We went to uni together. He was an arsehole back then, always getting in people's faces. Even accused me of stealing the girl he liked.' Andrew had the look of someone who was withholding the punchline.

'Did you?' Lexie held her breath, hoping for a no.

'Hardly. She was... *is* gay. Parker just couldn't see that.'

Lexie laughed and sipped her coffee. 'I even considered throwing in the job then and there.'

'Don't do that.'

'I won't. Not yet, anyway. Got a car to pay for. Rent, too.'

His short laugh was followed by a searching look.

'Forgive me?'

'No.' Lexie's response was fast, but backed by a teasing smile.

'Pardon?'

'In my family when you say sorry, you have to give the person a hug. It's a rule.'

'I like that rule.' He moved to her, folded his arms around her, and drew her close. She relaxed against his chest, closed her eyes and listened to the steady beating of his heart.

Without thinking of what she was doing, her fingers grazed his back in circles and she heard his intake of breath, felt his heartbeat quicken. His hand lifted and brushed her hair away from her face, and his lips, warm, hot, soft, pressed onto her forehead, as he breathed her in.

A shy cough broke the moment and they pulled apart like guilty teenagers. Lexie reached for a glass of water to hide her flushed cheeks. The waitress set down their food – share plates of scallops, sweetcorn croquettes and wild mushrooms – with a knowing smile, but didn't linger.

'Well, that worked as well as a cold shower,' Andrew muttered.

Lexie spluttered into her glass.

'Hey, saying it like it is.' The cheeky smile was back, his eyes teasing.

She matched his gaze. 'Maybe one of these days there'll be no need for that cold shower.'

Oh God. Tell me I didn't just say that out loud.

Lexie lazed in bed with her sheet kicked aside, and debated the merits of getting up or lying in. A Saturday lie-in would be well-deserved after the busy week she'd had, but considering summer was showing no sign of slinking off into the distance, perhaps it would be best to walk before it got too hot. Lexie was a long way off being able to run up the stairs at Point Peron like Andrew, but she'd been working on her fitness for the past month.

Andrew. All thoughts of fitness were forgotten as she imagined his face, his voice, the feel of his arms around her, and the taste of his mouth on hers. She reached for the photo she'd printed out at work, giggling as she recalled his reaction when he'd found it marking a page in the book she'd been reading.

'I remember this photo shoot,' he'd grinned.

'Don't remind me.' She'd coloured instantly, remembering the way her skirt had blown up in front of him.

'I have to admit, it is rather a nice memory. And your face is as red as those tiny, lacy things you were wearing.'

She'd swatted him with her book for that one.

God, I miss him.

It had been three weeks since she'd seen Andrew. Since they'd made up at Rustico, she'd only seen him one weekend before he was called up north to deal with fallout from the oil spill. Every night at eight-thirty they talked on the phone, sharing the highs and lows of their day. On Lexie's suggestion, they emailed what she dubbed 'Five Things Lists', revealing their five favourite sounds, places, songs and more, with a different theme each day. It was like an old-fashioned courtship with distance as the ever-present chaperone. A great way to get to know each other without rushing into things, but Lexie wouldn't have minded getting to know Andrew with a few more kisses and sunset walks thrown into the mix.

Kisses. I miss his kiss.

She sighed and threw her legs over the side of the bed. May as well get up. There was no way she was going to get back to sleep now. Not with thoughts of kisses invading her mind. She needed to do something to get her mind off Andrew. He'd told her he was coming home on Sunday morning and her mind was in countdown mode. One more sleep.

The Point of Love

A flash of white on the floor caught her eye. Kneeling down, ignoring the creak in her knees, she picked up an envelope that had fallen from her bedside table when she'd reached for the photo. Smiling, she fingered the envelope's contents – a voucher for a Rockingham Wild Encounters Swim with the Dolphins experience. It had been delivered to the office the day before, attached to a bunch of gerberas, and with a note requesting Lexie keep Sunday free. The gift had prompted a mad dash to the shops for new bathers, even though logic (and the company website) told her wetsuits would be provided. Vanity had proved too strong to resist in the end. Her mind drifted to wetsuits and Andrew... Andrew in a wetsuit... Andrew out of a wetsuit.

Stop!

Propping the voucher on her bedside table, she pottered into the lounge room and turned on the TV, hoping the noise would distract her from visions of taut muscles moulded into lycra, begging to be traced, memorised and traced again. Surfing the channels for a music station, Lexie paused on an ad for a Saturday night movie. Doors opening. A man with long hair striding into a dimly lit room. A voice like dark chocolate. A face like... Thor.

Very funny. Someone's having a laugh at my expense.

Waiting for the kettle to boil, she scrolled through her Facebook feed, noting she'd been tagged in a couple of posts by Mish. The first link took her to an image of a cookie cutter shaped like a hammer, with the word Thor on it. The second took her to an article about Thor Bjørklund, inventor of the cheese slicer. Lexie made a mental note to cover Mish's desk with post-its and clicked on the final link – a photoshopped image of Thor's head resting on a rose stem and the words "Every rose has its Thor". She rolled her eyes. Mish must have had a few too many wines last night. And thanks to that, she had Thor imprinted on her mind, right when she didn't need it.

Is that a hammer I can hear?

It took an insistent knock at the front door to banish her thoughts of muscle-bound gods in lycra splashing in the ocean. Lexie jumped and looked around furtively, as if someone had caught her mid-fantasy. Breathing out, refocusing her mind on less sensual matters like laundry and bikini waxing in the ten steps it took to reach the front door, she pulled the door open. And there he was. Not Thor. Andrew. Looking like a god in a fitted white t-shirt and jeans, while she looked like a banshee with her non-designer bed hair. Lexie stood, mouth agape, as Andrew's eyes raked her body, barely covered in too-short shorts and a crop top. She tried to pull her shorts down and succeeded only in revealing the soft curve of her belly. His mouth twitched.

'Aren't you going to invite me in?' That salted caramel voice. It sounded so much better in person.

'You're a day early,' she managed to squeak out, unlocking the security door with the hand that wasn't engaged in trying to cover her midriff. 'I wasn't expecting you.'

'I wanted to surprise you. Looks like I did.'

The Point of Love

'I'm a mess,' she began, giving up on the shorts and attempting to smooth her hair into something less explosive.

'You're perfect.' His mouth met hers before she could say another word.

Monique Mulligan

Thank you for reading *The Point of Love*. I hope you enjoyed it.

If you enjoyed it, please consider leaving an honest review on Goodreads or Amazon. Reviews can help readers find books and I would be grateful for your help. Thank you for taking the time to let others know what you thought.

If you'd like to know more about me, or connect with me online, please visit my webpage moniquemulligan.com, follow me on Twitter @writenote1, or like my Facebook page https://www.facebook.com/Eachdayagift/

This book was published by Serenity Press under its Serenity Romance imprint. If you'd like to see what else Serenity Press publishes, visit serenitypress.org

Monique Mulligan

Monique Mulligan has loved words from the moment she could use them. She earned the title of family chatterbox as a child, and once she could read, she devoured books with gusto.

A former **newspaper editor, journalist, children's curriculum writer** and **magazine editor,** Monique has had a varied career in writing. In 2011, she created Write Note Reviews, a blog that celebrates her love of reading. In 2012, she founded the successful Stories on Stage program at Koorliny Arts Centre, which features authors being interviewed in a theatre setting.

The Point of Love is Monique's first published fiction. She is now working on a full-length contemporary novel, as well as short fiction pieces.

Her website is www.moniquemulligan.com

www.ingramcontent.com/pod-product-compliance
Lightning Source LLC
Chambersburg PA
CBHW021137300426
44113CB00006B/461